Scripture quotations [marked NIV] taken from the Holy Bible,
New International Version Anglicised Copyright © 1979, 1984, 2011 Biblica
Used by permission of Hodder & Stoughton Ltd, an Hachette UK Company
All rights Reserved

A Book of Quotes

Two Trees Series

First published in 2022 by Dick Bell MBE

A Book of Quotes
by Dick Bell MBE

Contents

Prologue: A Book of Quotes.

Throughout my Christian years I have written things down. It was stimulated by the Baptist Pastor under whose wise and spiritual wing I was introduced to Jesus - Pastor Cecil Radford. I heard that he kept a scrap book, into which he wrote sayings, ideas, snippets that helped him on his way and that could be useful in some form or other in the future. So I copied his habit. I now have four scrap books. Three of them are full, and the fourth has many cuttings from magazines and places that I have yet to stick in.

Then there are sermons. When I was about one year old as a Christian, as I read through my Bible, the Lord gave me sermons – Three Points for teaching others. Those bullet points I also wrote down, and they have only come into use once. I looked at them one day to get inspiration for a sermon I was asked to preach, and all of them had lost their spiritual power and punch. I concluded that they had been for that day only. I haven't counted them, but there are hundreds. It helped with my spiritual understanding of God's wonderful written word at the time. If you like, they put clothes on the naked bodies of scripture verses.

Then there are the notes I wrote for my children and teenagers at Upcott. I still have them. Pages of them. I met a past student a year or so ago (now aged about 50) who said that he also had those notes in a bottom drawer somewhere. Still a resource, and available if and when needed.

The contents of this booklet are none of those.

These are new golden nuggets. They are culled only from the writings in the Two Trees Series, of which this is the antepenultimate Booklet, number 23. Few of them define any of the essays in any of the booklets, but they were part of each essay as the Lord opened up His doors and windows to me. Each is a "stand-alone" pearl. I pray that they will stimulate you, today's reader, and cause you to re-engineer your lifestyle under each searchlight as it pierces your soul.

None of them are direct quotes from the Bible. They are branches, leaves and flowers that have grown out from the trunk of scripture – if you can grasp the metaphor. God's truth is far, far bigger than the raw simplicity of the Bible writings. Every Christian will know that. God the Holy Spirit will explode a Bible verse to you at a moment in time, and teach you a truth or direct you to a task that is way beyond the simplicity of the words in front of you. My essays in these booklets are only extensions of many explosions. The quotes are jewels shining out from inside the writings, new leaves and new flowers on new twigs on new branches of God's wonderful tree Jesus.

I cannot recommend enough the practice of jotting down what God says to you in daily moments. If you are like me, you will never remember them unless you do. And, one day in your future on earth, you will surely be very grateful for their wisdom, a thing that you had long forgotten, but relevant to your "future today". After all, isn't that exactly what the Bible is? You are reading someone else's jottings, and they are pearls of wisdom and joy that swell your heart heavenwards, or correct your earthy mischiefs from further contaminatings.

This booklet has 7 chapters, consisting of 50 quotes each. That makes out to be 350 diamonds of eternal glory. (You will not do them all in one sitting). Then there is chapter 8, which at the time of writing this Prologue is not yet closed.

All of these bring glory to Jesus. He is the infinite reservoir of eternal goodies.

Chapter 1.

1. Democracy in Church kills the work of the Holy Spirit. Read that sentence again – and stop doing it.

2. I think the Christian life can easily be defined as one of "non-stop repentance from beginning to end."

3. I define *agapē* love as "Unconditional Acceptance".

4. It is worth my repeating here that Christianity is not a religion, it's a relationship.

5. Those who get the prompting do the job.

6. The practice of continually assessing whether a preacher is "sound" in his doctrine is the greatest hindrance to having God speak to us through a sermon.

7. Millions of people wrongly try to make Christianity an intellectual religion. It is neither intellectual nor a religion. It is Revelation.

8. God's appointing carries God's anointing, regardless of every other ability consideration.

9. Ephesians chapters 1 and 2 are all plural. I bet you've always interpreted them as singular.

10. I really do not accept a philosophy current today that "All roads lead to God." But I do subscribe to the view that "Many roads lead to Jesus," where "Only Jesus leads to God." Indeed, because all humans are unique, it occurs to me that that is the number of roads that are possible that lead to Jesus.

11. We humans divide things up as fractions of a whole. So we would tend to analyse God as part this, part that, part the other. But He is not. He is all this, all that, and all the others.

12. Jesus did not become a man to demonstrate how great man is or could become. He came to demonstrate how great God is.

13. The Holy Spirit lives universally, knows individually, and is available eternally to introduce anyone to Jesus.

14. Your stark choice is forgiveness or punishment. Both are Just. To ignore sin is injustice.

15. Time kills everything you have done; death cements it. Actually, every yesterday is dead. The world and all that is in it has only been put there to keep you alive until you find Jesus.

16. If you cling to shadows for your security, you become a shadow yourself.

17. Christian money should always be circulating. If you don't empty your bucket regularly, how can you expect God to keep on filling it?

18. Have you ever considered the *details* of Matt 7:21-23?

19. What do you make of the four-year leaders – those who stay in one church for a short time and then move on? How can they possibly have an effective ministry? Is it a career they are looking for? So what then would be their calling – into a professional priesthood? So what are they doing now – *practicing* on a congregation?

20. All local Churches are sub-standard. You'll not find a perfect one anywhere in the world.

21. What are Spiritual Butterflies? People who flit from Church to Church to find "one that suits them". Think of it – those who can't stand a particular Church and flit like butterflies will never find one to their liking until they end up in their own Church of one. Themselves.

22. Some children are terrified of church because they've seldom been in one.

23. If the church you lead is not changing, it is not growing, and you are not walking with the Lord. Denominational churches are in greatest danger of that.

24. If you don't care for people, no one will ever follow you. One does not need ability of any kind to be able to love other people.

25. But the charisma from the Lord lives and dies with the leadership position. The anointing comes with the appointing.

26. Surrendering to the laws of the universe enables individuals to flourish and grow; rebelling against them is guaranteed to bring disaster and death. Thus, if you stop eating or drinking, you die. The more people rebel against His (God's) laws, the more they invite disaster. No one can successfully swim against the flow of the universe. "*If a man remains in me and I in him, he will bear much fruit; apart from me you can do nothing.*" (John 15:5). That is a further eternal and unchanging law of the universe, and is the only way a human being can "bear much fruit". That is, for his life to be eternally and bountifully successful.

27. But now the Holy Spirit has been sent right across the earth. He has access to everyone because all the barriers which separate man from God have been dealt with by the one God-Man Jesus.

28. God does not argue or discuss – He only tells.

29. There is no such thing as a conventional human being.

30. It is impossible for evil ever finally to prevail over good.

31. If you translate "temptation from satan" into "testing from God", you will get a better perspective on how to handle it.

32. In existence there are only two "things", only two places to live, only two possibilities. There is either God or "me".

33. We become such good channels of His grace that we become redeemers like Jesus. We take on the Family likeness because we have taken on the Family ways.

34. I have to die to myself and my independence to become one with God, a mirror image reversal of Adam, who died to God to become independent.

35. Living by faith is much cheaper than living by calculation.

36. God sees straight and true. Man sees in bent or pecked lines and dimly (or through a glass darkly!)

37. Visionaries let the Lord build houses and cities. Watchmen do many things in vain. (Psalm 127).

38. Jesus not only learned what God wanted by being led all the time to do right, but also by learning what God did not want through temptations.

39. Many Christians believe that to obey man's Laws is to please God. That is never true.

40. All Law, divine and human, has been replaced by obedience to God the Holy Spirit.

41. Many Christians hunt for miracles when the normal will do perfectly. When the normal cannot provide, then is the time to ask God for a miracle. But, if you get what I am driving at, both are miraculous.

42. He does not coerce me to follow Him, even though He certainly has the capacity to do so. He *invites* me to follow His ways; He tells me His ways are the best possible in His universe; but love never coerces, never forces, only invites.

43. Jesus builds faith, not condemns failure. *Law* breeds failure, and loves the condemnation it generates. We are not under Law, but under Grace.

44. Every choice we make governs our destinies. We are and ever will be the sum of all our choices.

45. God is not counting sins, He is counting acts of faith.

46. To know that God has a future and a hope planned for us beyond death, and will carry us through this land of the dying until we reach the land of the living is a thing of great comfort to all us struggling followers.

47. Note that Jesus did not do what He thought was right, as many of us do. He did what God thought was right.

48. If you are thinking ordinarily, as every other human being thinks, you are living in sin. The mind governed by the Flesh is *dead*, or, more accurately, *death*. The mind governed by the Flesh is God's enemy – hostile to God. It *cannot* please God.

49. Now I am simply single-mindedly helping Jesus to rescue the rest of mankind. And, from that, eventually, the cosmos.

50. Whether I like it or not, I am fighting on God's side in a war I didn't choose to be in. I have an unavoidable part to play in bringing the goodness and glory of heaven to a dark world.

Chapter 2.

1. We all do much better with God than without Him.

2. An evolutionist is going to struggle to determine where universal mathematical laws originated. "It just does" is not good enough.

3. So, each of us must answer this question: "Why should God let me into His heaven?

4. I think that "Sin" can adequately summarise the whole history of earth and time.

5. God just wants people to love Him unconditionally. That will enable Him to love them back unconditionally.

6. "Doing" is not "being".

7. Concerning God, I don't have to be important. Only willing.

8. Walking with Jesus leaves a beautiful snail trail behind us.

9. To be faithful to Jesus every day leaves a wholesome reputation.

10. The only hidden agenda we are permitted is Jesus.

11. Heaven and earth are God's to share, not man's to earn.

12. None of us are bodies. We are souls, housed in bodies.

13. God's Grace enables the speaker to be clean, the message to be appropriate, and the receiver to be receptive.

14. We live in a dead world, a dead earth, a dead cosmos, and in dead bodies.

15. There will be no end to evil as long as any one of Adam's race still exists.

16. At the root of every human life is the desire to be good, and the longing to be loved.

17. God's will is only found in unity.

18. Democracy – the rule of the majority – is alien to the Bible, alien to God, and (I say boldly) sin. Democracy is the best philosophy of Government that *man* can conjure up. And now see what Democracy has led to – everyone having their own strong political opinions, and wanting everyone else to agree with *me*. The result – chaos.

19. The hassles don't change; we do.

20. So, what is a bad day? Answer: one in which you have not talked to Jesus enough in its on-going minutes.

21. Jesus has *koinōnia* (fellowship, participation) with everything we are and have from now on into eternity for ever.

22. Jesus is treading a very delicate line between giving us the very best possible in the universe and allowing us to choose the very worst possible in the universe.

23. Sitting in God's lap, I can pray effectively, strategically and confidently to change things of earth. Human logic is irrelevant. Earthen impossibilities cease to be impossible and are also irrelevant. I am not swayed by what I see, what I hear, what I think, what is clearly logical. God can change *all* things for good. Heaven is the reality of the universe. Earth definitely is not!

24. Christians are very expensive people.

25. Saying "No" to God is a self-inflicting injury.

26. Failure is a fact. So is forgiveness, and is readily available.

27. A Christian is someone in whom Jesus resides, and through whom Jesus lives.

28. God's laws are *living*; they arrive with Jesus. Man's laws are dead; they are inflexible; they are "things".

29. Goodness gets rewards and badness gets consequences.

30. Doing good without faith in Jesus is, compulsorily, sin.

31. All goodness in the whole of existence comes directly from God (James 1:17).

32. I have to reject the way the whole world thinks and acts - to swim against the river.

33. Everything that the Divine family does, it does it *together*. It loves together. It forgives together. It redeems together. It laughs together. It suffers together.

34. Just as each of our own children is a fragment and function of its parents, and share in their human DNA, so each human being born from above by the Holy Spirit is a fragment and function of Jesus, and shares in His divine DNA.

35. From our perspective, we *dare not* be left behind.

36. We are at the beginning of all things.

37. I will *inherit* the earth, but still never *own* any of it. Mine to use, but never mine to possess. We are only stewards of Jesus' possessions.

38. Time is merely recycling dust.

39. To do anything outside of God is to fail.

40. Every human destiny is the fulfilment of personal choices.

41. Sin and death are One Thing – two sides of the same coin. The cause and the consequence of eternal separation from all that is God are One Thing.

42. God can deal with us backwards because of what He knows of us forwards. Our past can be blessed because our future is divine, even though we never deserved the blessing at that time.

43. God gives to each of us, while still on earth, the blessings or the curses that His final judgement defines our lives as.

44. How we use our Now time is the key to the eternal definition of our lives.

45. Christians are twice unique. Once as a human being. The second with a "one-off" spiritual part (or section) of Jesus Christ, that uniquely complements and thereby uniquely completes our unique humanity.

46. I have to stop seeing myself as a son of Adam with a covering of Christianity; I am a Son of God with a covering of Adam's inadequacies.

47. Jesus the blueprint, each redeemed human the infinitely unique repeat.

48. We live only in Now. Beware yesterday, it is often full of regrets. Beware tomorrow, it is often full of anxieties and fears. Find God's peace Now, and all our yesterdays and all our tomorrows will also be full of peace.

49. Jesus' death on the cross was an obedient act of disobedience.

50. To include God impacts everything we do with eternal life.

Chapter 3.

1. Timelessness (after death) compulsorily means that none of us will ever change again.

2. Those "in Jesus" must also be "in God", because God is One.

3. The offer closes the moment any of Adam's descendants leave earth and die. That is when all deaths either remain eternal or remain eternally defeated.

4. That which has no eternal initiation has no eternal existence.

5. Fear is faith in satan.

6. All Christians on earth are half-cooked.

7. God is very gentle. But please do not mistake His tolerance for His approval.

8. My life is limited, but what there is of it is a channel through which God has access to this part of the world which I occupy.

9. Doctors will never be without a job to do on earth.

10. "Self" is a soul cancer. From birth.

11. God will provide opportunities every day for all those who are willing to talk about Him.

12. The harshest of tests produces the greatest of rewards.

13. For any of us to select unity with God instead of independence from God is to be lavished with such blessing that no tongue can tell of the infinite magnificence of it. Those who retain their independence have all the blessings they will ever have from earth. There are no more. There is no other.

14. Redeemed mankind cement the divine unity.

15. God's purpose, plan and way is that He should do all the suggesting, and we should do all the work.

16. The spirit realm is everywhere, not somewhere.

17. Adam voluntarily selected death, and bequeathed death to every human being. Jesus voluntarily selected death to offer redemption from death to every human being.

18. Jesus had no death in His body throughout His life, so that God could make death in Jesus' body the cornerstone of redemption at the cross.

19. Heaven and earth are God's to share, not man's to earn.

20. God has given us death so that we might choose to embrace Life.

21. Jesus was holy in spirit, soul and also in body. He came as the complete package. Actually, He is the only complete package in the universe.

22. God is making the impossible possible through Jesus. From inside out. It would be even more impossible from outside in.

23. God is too big to see, but small enough to hear.

24. It is far better to be a lowly servant in heaven than a king in hell.

25. To redeem man cost God everything He had.

26. The old man (Adam) was to rule over this old earth. The new Man is to construct a new earth from inside the Trinity. Jesus and His redeemed ones are the New Adam, the second Adam, the new mankind, the perfect mankind, the redeemed mankind, the divine mankind.

27. Now God works inside me in the same way that the Trinity work inside each other. We have become integral with God the Trinity's lifestyle.

28. All death is a separation. It is the opposite of "unity". Rather, and perhaps more fundamentally, all separation is a death.

29. He can become the internal assurance of eternal dimensions. Jesus *never fails*.

30. There is no joy greater than walking with Someone who is perfect in everything, especially relationships.

31. The mechanisms of birth are never a work of those born. In our case, to be begotten of God is a divine work of the Holy Spirit.

32. The good and forgiveness people refuse on earth they will also refuse after death when stark reality confronts them with clarity. Anyway, the offer closes at death.

33. God, who knows the end from the beginning, chooses those who choose Him in their lives.

34. Because God is fair, He gives everyone the opportunity.

35. Everyone chooses their own hell or their own heaven. That is, with God or away from Him. To love Him more than themselves, or to love themselves more than Him.

36. Parents are responsible for knowing what is the right way to live on planet earth.

37. Don't mess with the rules! Don't mess with the Word of God!

38. Not only was Jesus perfect, the pattern for His life was the perfect blueprint for every life on earth.

39. Work never ends.

40. "Live by the Spirit" says our Bibles (Gal 5:16). That is the only way to keep our eternal fire refuelled, stoked up and burning bright.

41. If he did not place his trust in the eternal God, he has no eternal significance. Nor will you or I have, if we do not secure our life's unique treasures in God's eternal bank.

42. "Out there" is the only place to do it. "By the Spirit" is the only way to do it.

43. To live by the scriptures is *not* God's way of living the Christian life; living by the Spirit is. Living by the scriptures is not spiritual freedom. It is Biblical bondage. They are in bondage to the scriptures. The letter kills, but the Spirit gives life. Not by the scriptures, but by the Holy Spirit *through* the scriptures. And then everywhere else.

44. The Holy Spirit has to make us feel bad before we can feel good. Only Jesus can provide the means of being good. God's solution is a transformed human being.

45. Restoration required a cross. And agony. And hell. And death. And ultimate abject transparency – naked, bloody, exposed, personal, infinite. God died eternally so that love could win eternally.

46. That cry rings out throughout the millennia of time – "I love every one of you. See what I *did* to tell you." We all need to be cuddled in the arms of the God who loves.

47. God is permanently manipulating time.

48. I suppose I could summarise heaven and hell this way: heaven is an everlasting state of forgiveness: hell is an everlasting state of punishment for unforgiveness.

49. It will be your faith in His words in your mind that will enable you to be fruitful in your talking ministry.

50. God has a definition of sin: "Everything that has been done without Jesus is sin. Everything."

Chapter 4.

1. Living on earth is learning heaven.

2. So, walking daily with Jesus increases our understanding of the Man who is God; we get nearer the reality of the Almighty.

3. People who followed Jesus changed the world (rather than maintaining the world in the same direction that they found it in when they entered it).

4. There are many very clever, gifted and intelligent people who rise to the top of their professions and achieve nothing eternal with their lives. That's what I call wasted lives.

5. People whose lives are separated from God are fighting the whole universe. Everything about the creation works against them.

6. Riches on earth is satan's devious way of trying to by-pass God's good promises, and get them in some other way and time than God designed.

7. To rest does not mean to stop work; it means to stop striving while working, and keep our restfulness in Jesus.

8. We exist simply because God is pleased that we should. It is our absolute glory that we are completely dependent on the Lord for everything.

9. All the evil we witness on earth has been stimulated by demon spirits but perpetrated by human beings. Satan has no power to change that order of things.

10. But God's ways are not ours. Jesus had to be nothing in everything, so that His Father could be everything in everything.

11. Please understand this: this first earth was created perfect in every respect. But selfishness entered it, first through satan, then into man. God cannot let that happen again in His new earth.

12. Just like Jesus had to bleed to redeem us, we are going to have to bleed to qualify for His Heaven.

13. Jesus made the earth and He knows the very best way to live in the world that He has made. His way and His world are one thing.

14. His *doing* is always practical and always perfect, and He belongs in His doing. Being invariably leads to Doing in God's economy.

15. What I have to learn is to Be while I Do. That's what God does, so that's what I must do.

16. Praise God for the Cross, which continually enables Jesus to detox my history.

17. "The Flesh" is me living an ordinary human life without Jesus. If that is what I do, my whole life is lost. I am a dead man; not Living but existing.

18. Do you see – if **by the spirit** you put to death the misdeeds of the body, you will live? If you put to death the misdeeds of the body by your own self-control, you will not only die, you will fail.

19. So, just how much has the Holy Spirit had an influence to change our normal ordinary human life? How different are our lives from that of our neighbours – apart from us going to Church and they don't?

20. We cannot see, hear, touch, feel or taste the Kingdom of God, much less God Himself. He insists on this really rather unnatural and bizarre device called faith.

21. So God has incorporated hiddenness into the fabric of earth. Presumably that is because His humility insists on not pushing Himself forwards at any time or in any way.

22. Can a "thing" (actually, they say "a nothing") make such a complicated being as an animal?

23. God has reproduced Himself in human form so that His existence is unmistakably obvious; Jesus was perfect in everything He did.

24. There are two books we can read concerning Him – Nature and the Bible. Nature is perfect and complete and anyone with only a tiny bit of knowledge can understand that and stand in awe and wonder at it. The Bible, on the other hand, has to be read.

25. What do *you* find is the most consistent and most reliable thing in which you have placed your trust that has the greatest guarantee of fulfilment for ever?

26. God's plan is to make mankind ruler over the new, better, perfect, replacement earth and heavens.

27. Regardless of the tasks we perform, in our daily round or common task, learning how to perform these in a way that gets God's full approval will lead us to performing it perfectly and for ever next time around on the Second Earth.

28. Not only is this earth a testing ground, it is a training ground.

29. God banished him (satan) to earth (the First Earth, this one) for the express purpose of giving us as much hassle as he possibly could. He is here to tempt us and to test us. We are being purified through suffering (Heb 2:10).

30. Jesus came down to carry His lovers up. Everyone else goes down. Earth is the testing ground, the middle place of choice.

31. Satan relishes man-centredness. It keeps men away from God. That's got to be the major reason why so many clever people think God is a myth. Do they know they have been duped?

32. And the Bible adds that 'Love covers over a multitude of sins.' The greatest of which is division, and the second of which is mind-centred intellectualism masquerading as Christianity.

33. That is Him in there, not me in there, giving me ideas and directions.

34. Christianity is a love-in between Jesus and you, you and Jesus. Stop thinking yourself and your intelligence are so marvellous. Your brain is wonderful; you are not.

35. We are being acted upon by the overwhelming love that permeates the Trinity, that is barely resistible, that engulfs everything we are and have. We have been caught up by the dynamo of the universe, the *raison d'être* of all creation, the purpose of all things. Being "in Christ" means being crushed along with Him.

36. If we are to be like Jesus, like God, embrace love, then the first thing we have to have happen to us is to die. *"Whoever wants to be my disciple must deny themselves and take up their cross daily and follow me."* (Luke 9:23).

37. We are destined for destruction of all of self. If you cannot take the cost, you will pay the price yourself in hell.

38. God has surrounded us, grabbed us, and we cannot escape the driven dynamo of His love.

39. We are all living by faith daily anyway; now, we must make that faith a Faith into Jesus. Jesus is the only solid there is in this created universe. All else is shadow.

40. Anything I do without Jesus is a total waste of time, belongs in hell and is a dead work. Faith enables Life. Only God's Life is eternal, and it cannot be found without Faith.

41. We live in eternity – the ever-present Now. But time has been created by God from the beginning in order to make everything outside of Now deeply uncertain. I and Jesus live together only in Now.

42. Both fear and anxiety use faith as a vehicle for their existence, but always into darkness and negatives. Satan is forced to use faith to get people to follow him.

43. Men, so full of their own intelligence and pride, think they are better informed than the God of the Bible is.

44. I, in my human nature, am hostile to God, *cannot* please Him and am living in death. (Rom 8:5-8).

45. Being an architect (for example) has never galvanised Christianity in anyone.

46. Simply, to do the will of God right Now is to fulfil all Laws in the universe.

47. Many people define a Christian as one who keeps every human law perfectly. Bad opinion.

48. I own nothing in heaven, and possessing anything on earth is plain stupid. Why try grasping or collecting shadows?

49. The privilege of being a human being has the added consequence of being indestructibly permanent.

50. Let the rich give their riches, the poor give their service and all of us give our time.

Chapter 5.

1. When anyone is reconciled to heaven, everything becomes beautifully clean and good.

2. I am Jesus' representative here on earth, and what bothers me bothers Him.

3. *Disappointment* can never be part of God's Kingdom. *"For we live by faith, not by sight,"* (2 Cor 5:7). From that perspective, Time is an enemy. Another day whereby prayers have not yet been answered breeds unbelief, engineered by satan. Away with you!

4. We are spirit beings, whether we know it or not, whether we discern it or not, whether we like it or not, whether we care or not. We are whom we have been born to be.

5. Those who accept expand upwards. Those who reject shrink downwards.

6. All evil throughout the cosmos is quarantined to earth.

7. The only people who can qualify for heaven are those who have lived perfect lives from birth to grave – or those who have been forgiven.

8. There are those who choose to retain their independence, and live for ever outside of God, and those who choose dependence and live for ever inside God.

9. God creates and sustains - we and the creation use.

10. We were all born Dead and dying, twice dead.

11. If I, now, as an older, wiser, more mature Christian man, were to forgive the stupid younger me for what I did when I was being stupid, I would set myself free from the guilt of what I did.

12. There is only one goodness in the universe, and that is God's. That is because God is absolutely unselfish. Man is always selfish, so all his goodness is bad.

13. God is not going to change His plan for this universe because you or I don't like it. Or don't want it.

14. If I don't need to do something I had planned to do right now, but do what He is prompting me to do, even though I hadn't thought of doing it and don't particularly want to do it, it always turns out the best thing I could have done.

15. I, who am strictly limited to Here and Now, am living eternally and contributing eternally to the running of the universe simply by saying Yes and doing it.

16. Repentance allows Jesus in to engineer the transformation of our basic natures.

17. The Son of God had to suffer. Thus *all* sons and daughters of God have to suffer.

18. One redeemed human soul is greater in sum than the whole of this present universe put together.

19. The privilege of living brings the certainty of judgement.

20. Heaven is absolutely impossible for any human being with the wrong shape.

21. So, physical and spiritual. That had to be man's shape. We are the only beings in the universe with that shape.

22. I no longer *work* to be saved – Jesus has completed all the salvation necessities.

23. I no longer ask God to bless what I have been doing – I do what He has already decided to Bless.

24. I am just like God in my character because I am declared by God to be one of His Sons.

25. Any petrol station (i.e. Christian Church) will do for a top up, no matter who is selling the petrol.

26. We belong to Jesus, are in Jesus, are fully in Him, are full of Him, have no other considerations, are sitting relaxed inside His fullness all day and every day, merely letting the overflow pour through us.

27. We are extensions of God on earth.

28. We do not need to strive for anything that God has already given us.

29. Most of us lost the battle and became character cripples all through our lives.

30. Many people die bitter and negative old failures.

31. Even Christians can die bitter old failures, characterised more by sin than by triumph.

32. No sin can be forgiven by God unless it is first confessed.

33. Only Jesus can remove satan's implants, and engineer God's implants – God's spiritual ways - within us.

34. Nobody by trying can be righteous enough. At least righteous as God wants it.

35. Jesus is not religious. He is real. He transcends heaven and earth, connecting both.

36. Jesus completes His philosophies of two thousand years ago by enabling Him to accomplish them in you and me today.

37. Sin is rampant amongst all of mankind, the fact of which we are all well aware. We are born in sin, we "do" sin, we die because of sin. We are all addicted to sinning. There are no human exceptions.

38. The renewal of our spirits by His Spirit begins to bite into our selfishness inside.

39. My soul gets changed. Everything about what I think, say and do on earth becomes what Jesus wants me to think, say and do on earth.

40. The spiritual part of our natures means that, like the angels, we too are indestructible. We are eternal creatures.

41. To obtain anything, we have to lose everything.

42. Only the nobodies get promoted.

43. "Things" do not have ability. Things are; they don't do.

44. Without Jesus' rescue, we have no rescue.

45. Jesus' kind of Life is incomparable, irreplaceable and irreversible.

46. We cannot possibly qualify for God's *approval*: the only thing we can possibly qualify for is God's mercy.

47. The perspective that Jesus' listeners did not have was that the redemption was so absolute and so complete that no one had any need ever again to *do* anything to please God or to do His will on the earth.

48. He provides the ideas, the availability, the ability, the motivation, everything. Nothing is hard work when God works inside us. God has completed everything, completely.

49. Of course God has *got* to make it difficult for us – He knows what inheritance He has planned for us.

50. He does not give me superhuman eyesight: He gives me superhuman insight.

Chapter 6.

1. There has hardly if ever been one day I have lived on earth when I have been completely satisfied that I have behaved wisely, acted courageously, thought cleanly, or spoken kindly. I am one of those in the quote above who will be saved *"as one escaping through the flames"* – that is, by the skin of my teeth and only by God's forgiving grace.

2. It is not possible for goodness of any kind to originate from any other source than Jesus in this universe.

3. There's none so blind as those who prefer to remain in their own hell.

4. The full sequence? Anarchy, law, repentance, surrender to Jesus, being born of the Holy Spirit, water baptism, Holy Spirit baptism, effective Christian living, heaven. That is what God has gifted to have happen to every single human being on earth. Never be content with less than the very best that God has provided.

5. Those who, during their lifetime on earth, have given no consideration to the spirit and eternal realm, end up with the spirit realm returning the favour and giving them no consideration either.

6. God has an unlimited supply of hassle that He can personally apply to each of us differently so that we might come to rely on Him more and more.

7. So, God calling Himself I AM suddenly gave Israel a God of continuity. What He did for Abraham He can now do for us.

8. So His guidance right now perfectly fits into my Now situation, my Now activity, my Now availability, my Now planned pathway in life (Eph 2:10), my own future and what the rest of the universe is doing at this Now time.

9. The single alternative to surrendering to Jesus while on earth is surrendering to hell when we leave earth. Hell is a self-inflicted injury.

10. No one will go to hell unless they have rejected Jesus while they have opportunity here on this beautiful earth. Anyone can choose heaven by choosing Jesus.

11. What normal people normally believe, that if their goodness is more frequent than their badness here on earth, God will be kind to them and let them in to His heaven. That is never in the Bible.

12. When we gave up the sovereignty of running our lives to Jesus, He entered our lives on the inside. Satan was not replaced; he only took second place.

13. It is extraordinary how easily we hear satan's suggestions and temptations on our insides and how hard we find God's suggestions to hear.

14. Satan and his demons are strictly forbidden to force us to sin. They can tempt; but *we* have to make the decision to sin or not. God, on the other hand, has restricted Himself to the same limitation. He *will not* force us to obey Him. All choices I make are mine, and one day I will have to give an account for every one of them.

15. It has taken me a lifetime to emerge from Self and prefer (and therefore select) Holy Spirit direction.

16. He (Jesus) is the only human being in the universe who can help me please God at all times. You cannot. Neither can I for you.

17. Human education does not please God; that is not God's way of learning. What is? Revelation (according to my Bible). *God* teaches me everything I need to know about absolutely everything.

18. Only God contains Life. I thought that I was learning great stuff as I read my Bible. I wasn't: I was *being taught it* by the Holy Spirit.

19. Like a little boy pulling the wings and legs off a fly while it is still alive just for his personal pleasure, so mankind has poisoned and polluted God's good earth and fouled it for ever, just for our personal pleasure.

20. What God was looking for was a bunch of physical/spiritual creatures who would be prepared to go through any kind of trouble to qualify to help Him run His New Heavens and New Earth for Him. So today's earth is God's "School of Hard Knocks" for heaven.

21. Fitting in with it (God's strategic Plan) seems to me to be the most important thing a human being can ever consider doing. What is your strategic plan for your life after you die?

22. That is the initial transformation that makes us a Christian. I give up my own way and choose Jesus' way. I renounce the ways of Knowledge, Good and Evil and choose God's way only. No longer me; now only Jesus.

23. Christians do not *think through* their Christians lives – they learn by Revelation from Heaven; they live by Revelation from Heaven; they "walk by the Holy Spirit"; they live by the fruit of the Tree of Life, and no other way.

24. By God's immeasurable Grace, perfect wisdom and immaculate timing, we have access to the Tree of Life, by which alone we can and must live on earth today.

25. During our time on earth, God is presenting us continually with His perfect guidance, love and forgiveness. After our time on earth, He will present us with His assessment of us, His Judgement.

26. Every act of faith in Jesus' promptings by you is cosmically unique – a new creation; and eternal. Nothing is lost from any Christian's faith in Jesus.

27. It is what is going on in the *inside* that all of us need to focus on, so that we do not consequently do rash or wicked deeds on the outside. External actions always have an internal trigger.

28. We know to do good, but our bodies want to do otherwise. We all also know every moment that we surrender to the cravings of our Flesh (or our own little ideas), and choose it or them rather than the suggestions that the Lord is making.

29. Christians have the powerful advantage of God living in our insides; He not only suggests righteousness, but, if asked, produces it in us. Each of us has fleshly weaknesses.

30. "*Everything that is not of faith is sin.*" (Rom 14:23). That is the best definition of Flesh that I can find.

31. God has decided that the only human being in the universe who has His full approval is Jesus. Jesus has been perfect and fully obedient throughout His existence, and especially in His 33 years on earth.

32. Jesus has made provision for every Christian to know His suggestions in every moment of every day by having Himself, and the whole Trinity, living inside us. We should make decisions like They do – together, and of one heart and one mind with Them. All else is Flesh.

33. If, today, you are not a better person than you were yesterday, yesterday's lessons were valueless.

34. God's purpose, plan and way is that He should do all the suggesting, and we should do the work. He will never change that arrangement. Then all of mankind's work on earth would be God initiated. Therefore perfect. And unique through each individual. The life of Jesus on earth is the kind of result God is looking for.

35. You have chosen to enter the Kingdom of God and surrender your life to following Jesus. Death to everything you were and want is the inevitable result. You are in deep trouble. Along with me.

36. Law was God's perfect way of highlighting our sinful inabilities by continually comparing us to a standard of perfection. *"Law is our paidagōgos (whipping slave) to lead us to Christ"*. (Gal 3:24).

37. He (God) is putting suggestions of goodness into every mind, in much the same way that satan is putting ungodly or unrighteous suggestions into human minds daily.

38. We have no original goodness. Only Jesus is good. We are all utterly dependent on Him for all things. That is the way God has always wanted the universe to be and to run.

39. The desires of the flesh – what our bodies crave if we let them indulge – is an enemy of what the Holy Spirit is prompting on our insides.

40. Every behaviour pattern that is in discord with God's behaviour pattern – *that* is sin.

41. Every moment in time requires a decision from me, and I either do what I have always done, or what I think I will do, or I engage Jesus in those momentary decisions and do what He suggests I should do.

42. Do not be deceived into thinking that nice people go to heaven because they are nice. They are not. Therefore they won't. *"Man looks at the outward appearance, but the Lord looks at the heart."* (1 Sam 16:7).

43. Many people we know are good, kind, law-abiding, generous and likeable people. Surely they qualify for heaven? Not according to my Bible. Every one of them would admit that they are not perfect, and certainly no one is.

44. All our good deeds can only be expressed inside the impenetrable box of sin. Sin is a condition – a state. All good that we know and do comes from a condition of independence. God describes that independence as sin.

45. The demonstration that God cares about mankind, and the proof that He penetrates the barrier is Jesus. God has come down to earth and got His hands dirty, so that He could change mankind from inside out by the way of love not law.

46. Jesus demonstrated a new way – total obedience to God through an intimate relationship with Him, because running by Law was self-effort which did not necessarily need God at all. Besides, *"The law made nothing perfect."* (Heb 7:19).

47. Man could still choose backwards, reversing his inherited rebellion. In an environment of complete goodness, choice had to include the alternative of evil; now, in an environment of complete evil, choice had to include the alternative of goodness.

48. Satan can only tempt after the manner of his own evil. There is no other kind of evil. The choice for all is simple – to love and serve God or to live independently of God.

49. God's kind of love needed to be voluntary. So both men and angels had to be given choice. Where there is no alternative, there is no choice.

50. Where God was perfectly capable of sorting everything out for Himself, He chose to have others – angels and man – to do it for Him. Then love would be both ways.

Chapter 7.

1. The uniqueness of each individual, under satan's control, forces us all to retain the isolation of independence. Segregated, we are filled with "Me, me, me." The uniqueness of each individual, under *God's* design control, leads us all to personal self-actualisation. Fulfilled, we prefer "Others, others, others".

2. This distinction is absolutely boundaried. No two humans think alike, desire alike, act alike, dream alike, react alike, or have similar talents or characters. Their uniqueness is total.

3. As an individual with my unique Character Signature, there is no other human being in the universe who can relate perfectly to me.

4. Jesus has the only location in the universe in which my soul can be fully satisfied. He is the only key to my unique padlock.

5. I either fulfil my design purpose for being alive, or I condemn myself for ever to be the only human being in the universe. I am "one of a kind".

6. So here is the truth of our personal and individual existence – why we are alive at all. We are created unique. Because we are unique, we either remain isolated on our own for ever, or get completed by Jesus and live with Him and His family for ever. There are no alternatives.

7. Without surrender and sacrifice there is no Christianity. Without Christ there is no heaven.

8. God also knows that this earth, and this earth only, is the one place where we will meet satan and his hordes of demons. Never again, after death, will a Christian meet a demon.

9. Regrettably, every non-Christian will go to bed with all the full company of demons in that eternal night that never has a dawn. Entry into man's eternal prison is of his own making – ending up there is a self-inflicted destiny, and entirely unnecessary.

10. Do you know what a "Custard Christian" is? It's one that gets upset over trifles.

11. Grace came before creation.

12. It was Jesus' cross that engineered, from God's perspective, that explosion of transformative power that works salvation into every nook and cranny of a human being, bringing the renovation that is necessary for heaven.

13. Every human being born on earth to Adam and Eve therefore inherited multi-functional death. They were, and are, all dead in their souls, their spirits and their bodies. Nothing about any human being born to mankind pleases God. God *loves* mankind, but does not approve of anything they do.

14. So they do good things, but never please God in doing them.

15. Without Jesus, none of us can say anything.

16. I have written before, and I repeat – there is *nothing* that any of us can do to contribute to our salvation. The engineering of it has been completely completed without us.

17. So all good that man does actually comes from God and is initiated by Him, but man thinks that he has initiated it himself (because man is unable to think any other way than selfishly).

18. We are in a constant struggle to rid ourselves of ourselves, even though Jesus has made us more ourselves than we could ever have been without Him.

19. To be like the Lord is His work in us, not our work in ourselves. To try to be like Jesus robs God of Grace.

20. To rest does not mean to stop work; it means to stop striving while working, and keep our restfulness in Jesus.

21. The making of happiness for others contrasts with the central core of the universe - to make God happy.

22. The Holy Spirit inside us aches for the holiness that is Father, and cries out that He, inside me, is being contaminated by self and sin, and pleads to be made whole and holy like Father is.

23. If we are to be like Jesus, like God, embrace love, then the first thing we have to have happen to us is to die. *"'Whoever wants to be my disciple must deny themselves and take up their cross daily and follow me."* (Luke 9:23).

24. All the juice must come out and flow away; we are destined for destruction of all of self. If you cannot take the cost, you will pay the price yourself.

25. What does God do with all those human beings He loves? If Jesus is an indicator, God crucifies them.

26. How can an individual be perfectly humble without another to whom He gives His all? That is why there *must* be a Trinity. To be perfectly humble requires one to give all perfectly. To give perfectly requires one to be perfectly empty. Without that circle there is no perfection.

27. God enabled and commissioned His servant satan to do everything he could to break every human being, to show man that sin never works, and to test man's love commitment for God.

28. We all deserve all the hassle we get. We do *not* deserve the redemption, forgiveness and grace of love that God freely offers us. But it is ours to have forever, if we would like to.

29. Oh what a foolish man I have been all my life! I'm far too talented for any eternal usefulness.

30. The *I* in me is God's worst enemy, the earth's worst enemy, the universe's worst enemy, and my own worst enemy. *I* am the greatest disaster the universe has ever known.

31. The two trees in the Garden of Eden were spiritual lifestyle activators exclusively made for mankind.

32. Our nothing opens space for His everything.

33. He gives back to us from His infinite store of excellence the exhilaration of experiencing what the Grace of Heaven can do when His Holy Spirit has full availability.

34. Only under God's direct authority can my birthed authority have an eternal destiny of goodness.

35. Now, every human descendant of Adam, personally, has the choice to retain his eternal uselessness, or surrender to the God of Jesus and reinstate his eternal usefulness.

36. God made man equal to Lucifer, at the top end of the creation order.

37. The Good News of Jesus Christ carries within itself seeds of its own reproduction, because it is always accompanied by Life through the Holy Spirit, to whom God has given the seeds of the Words of Jesus in the Oneness that is the Trinity. Jesus is the Word of God and the words of God.

38. Because God is God and always has the final say, that choice of ours makes us either the greatest shame the universe will ever know, or the greatest magnificence the universe will ever know.

39. In heaven, there will never be any scriptures. Nor forgiveness. Nor any tomorrows.

40. Satan is God's agent for good on this earth. (Work out why).

41. No man, by thinking or deciding, can rid himself of spiritual iniquities. Only God can do that. It has to be a divine deliverance.

42. The consequence of putting our brains to work in our daily lives is that we live lives alien to God, and darken everything we say and do with the devil's iniquities.

43. We sophisticated, educated Christians, think that we can live the Christian life with hardly any reference to the Holy Spirit; just read the scriptures and obey them. But God will not have it. He is insisting that we go back to living by the Holy Spirit, with minor check-ups from the scriptures.

44. Nothing from God is going to happen on earth unless or until we do it the Holy Spirit's way.

45. The written word of God *cannot* ever be the final arbitrator on Truth or behaviour. We must not take away that arbitration from the Holy Spirit, who alone on our earth has the handle for spreading truth to us. Jesus said so in John 16:13.

46. We can live without the scriptures. Most of us do anyway in our normal, everyday lives. But we *cannot* live without the Holy Spirit.

47. We think we are better off than the early Christians – we have the scriptures. But in fact we are far worse off. Our use of the scriptures is, mainly, fleshly. The early Christians were far better off; they were illiterate, and *only* had the Holy Spirit.

48. It does not matter how often we fail. What *really* matters to God is how often we believe and trust.

49. There is no other purpose of living on earth as a human being, but to learn the difference between Good and Evil. (The hard way).

50. We have to relinquish all of earth to embrace heaven.

Chapter 8.

1. It is the Father's good pleasure to give us the Kingdom. That was His only aim from the beginning of earth, and the only purpose for making the earth.

2. All mankind has been born into independence, inherited from Adam. All mankind has been born into pain.

3. All those born from above by the Holy Spirit into Jesus carry the full consequences of that redemption – Eternal Life. All those remaining in Adam still carry the consequences of their independence – Eternal Death.

4. The single purpose for creating an earth and all its environs was to produce a wife for God's Son Jesus, made up of human beings. That was, and still is, His only aim. Only His Love and Grace has enabled that to happen.

5. Truth, as in Jesus, is infinite in quality in its divisions down into comprehensible lumps.

6. Satan always misuses good to generate evil.

7. I have no credit without Jesus.

8. Everything outside of Him is none of my business and everything outside of me and Him are His responsibility only.

9. Indeed, everything that I do, even the simplest of domestic duties, becomes an extension of God's fulness.

10. Sonship in God is doing what THE Son (Jesus) was and did, for God has decided and determined that we should be *just like Jesus*.

11. We do not need to strive for anything that God has already given us.

12. I no longer *work* to be saved – Jesus has completed all the salvation necessities. I no longer ask God to bless what I have been doing – I do what He has already decided to Bless. I do not work *for* God – I work *from* God. I no longer ask God for the things He has promised – I simply receive them. Sonship, the concept behind this writing, is one of them. I *receive* my status of Son; I *receive* the full blessing of God; I *receive* the power through me to align my part of the universe with God's ways; I *receive* words of knowledge as God trusts me with them.

13. I am just like God in my character because I am declared by God to be one of His Sons.

14. We, like Jesus, do not let anything of the world affect us, but, in contrast, allow the fulness of God to impact the world through us by word and deed. We are extensions of God on earth.

15. Those in heaven will have two kinds of eternal existence – body and spirit. Those in hell will have only one.

16. Our bodies are merely a suitable device for transporting our souls, and our souls are responsible for allowing our bodies to do what they do.

17. Crucifixion and resurrection are the daily experience of every Christian.

18. Human bodies and souls are united in agreement – we love sinning.

19. How Jesus resisted sin for thirty-three years beats me. I have trouble doing it for one day. I find my body to be almost irresistible. That is one reason why I bow down and worship Him.

20. God's anger at the obscenity of independence had to be dealt with.

21. I do not work *for* God – I work *from* God. I no longer ask God for the things He has promised – I simply receive them.

22. The Holy Spirit can never be duplicated, not even by the Bible.

23. A personal relationship with the living God is unmissable, unmistakeable, distinctive, unambiguous, particular, clearly identifiable and evident.

24. Heaven is confined only to Jesus.

25. I am responsible to Him – He is responsible for me.

26. We have "fellowship" with Jesus' divinity and His humanity. We suffer with His sufferings. We are divine with His divinity.

27. The iniquity of self implodes and shrivels into the minute atrocity of one. Jesus *explodes* and becomes inclusive into the companionship and "fellowship" participation of all into One.

28. The Oneness of Me is exceedingly small. The Oneness of all in Jesus is exceedingly large.

29. The *I* in me has to be killed to make room for the *Us* in God to take over.

30. God is an "Us", and Jesus is going to have to include us in that "usness" of God.

31. God – the Trinity and apprentice me – are experiencing suffering and redemption together in our moments on earth.

32. The redemption that God engineered through Jesus on His Cross did far more than simply enable Him to forgive sin. It enabled Him to re-engineer mankind itself.

33. Without Jesus, no human being is any better than a demon of hell.

34. God had to reconstruct mankind completely if He was going to allow mankind to enter heaven as Jesus' bride and wife.

35. His cross redeemed everything.

36. His cry *"Finished"* on the cross is far more significant than His end of life. It cleansed the whole cosmos, wiping clean every aspect of existence that did not conform to God's goodness, grace and way of life.

37. You do realise, don't you, that anxiety and worry by any of us condemns God to be incompetent?

38. The Holy Spirit's humility is eternal. That contributes to why He is so cuddly towards those who continue to cultivate His company.

39. God's consistency is eternal.

40. God did not change His mind – He was determined to have mankind with Him in heaven. He simply changed His method.

41. There can be no multiplication without "motherhood". Womanhood through Eve carries the privilege for all multiplication in man, animals, and plants (Gen 3:20).

42. How strongly and ferociously we resist His efforts to do us good!

43. Jesus' sovereign decision was to delegate His sovereignty to His Father.

44. Therefore God had to punish Jesus infinitely with eternal death, therefore condemning the whole of Adam's race of human beings to eternal death. The whole of mankind was killed. All mankind was exposed by God as being unfit for continued existence.

45. The dregs of a condemned human could be the seed of transformation into a Son of God. The resurrection is a new creation – a new humanoid.

46. God, in His love, planted the "Tree of Sin" in Eden as the ultimate demonstration of the nature of divine love.

47. Deny him*self*. In the same way, we have to give up everything of Adam's version of humanity, so that we can embrace (be born into) Jesus' new version of humanity – living in perfect unity with the Triune God.

48. A *real* man (human being), a *complete* man, one that fulfils his design signature, is a man who is one with God and at complete peace with the God of heaven. There are no other types of human as designed.

49. Man and satan were an alliance of death together.

50. None of us has the capacity to imagine God's future capabilities.

51. It has always been the plan of God the Trinity to bring mankind into that position – of being part of God Themselves. God made man expressly to reign with Him in the Godhead alongside Jesus and the Holy Spirit. Today on earth we must realise that *we are* the beginning of all things.

52. Every descendant of Adam's are all sinful human beings.

53. Holy Spirit first, scripture second.

54. In life, grot first, glory second.

55. God, from His fullness, delights to give of His fullness. The only way to receive it is to receive it. Then give it away, because receiving what is not ours and that we have not earned is glorified in giving it away.

56. A crooked human being will get his eternal pleasure in crookedness that can never satisfy – an eternal unsatisfied satisfaction in eternal dissatisfaction.

57. Others have said that Jesus, as God, became a man in His incarnation. That, I think, is the wrong way round. I think that He was always a Man. Adam was made in His image, not the other way round.

58. The word "criticism" and the word "Christian" should never be seen together.

59. A creation that was designed to run on togetherness would never survive on selfishness.

60. No human being can ever be a success without God.

61. Do you see how impossible it is for any creature to live successfully outside their design parameters?

62. God here introduces the entanglement of death with love, and in that battle, Love always wins, because Love is a greater spiritual motivator for justice than righteousness is.

63. Walking with Jesus enables us to walk far better than the best the Law could provide.

64. Earth is far too shallow to have designed someone as complex as we are.

65. Years ago, I wanted to be free to sin. Now, in Jesus, I am free not to sin, and bathe in the luxury of absolute goodness.

66. The only things it cost us are the eternally tormenting nothingnesses of hell.

Epilogue.

Oh, the absolute wonder of it all! The Kingdom of Heaven is so full that it is inexplicable. There are understandings after understands, reconciliations after reconciliations, truths after truths, pleasures after pleasures, joy after joys and peace that surpasses the understanding. All of it is irrational because the Kingdom of God is far beyond reason.

Have you ever asked any of the questions: "Why does God love? Why does He reconcile? Why does He do the beautiful things He does?" There is no rationale that can give a rational answer. He simply loves to bless.

He loves to straighten what is crooked. Why? Because He knows that crookedness always fails, always darkens, always destroys, always misaligns with everything. It is like trying to stand against a 150 mile-an-hour tornado. The whole universe fights against crookedness. Don't the crooked ever long to live in peace and stop fighting what they know to be right, straight, loving and kind? Why fight against a love that reconciles? Why insist on destruction that only ever destroys? Why break apart that which is only useful when whole? Why does satan relish destroying everything good in the universe? Why does man? There is an addictive power in delighting to destroy. We see that in dictators using their war machines to grab other people's territory. We see that in dictators lining their own pockets with money that should have gone to the poor to alleviate their poverty. And then they die and the money is no longer theirs. Stupid. The drive is pure demonic. Satan fills the heart of man to steal, kill and destroy. And man *loves* it. It gives him wonderful, sadistic pleasure. Actually it gives him *eternal* pleasure. A crooked human being will get his eternal pleasure in crookedness that can never satisfy – an eternal unsatisfied satisfaction in eternal dissatisfaction.

How beautiful is the God of all things beautiful. At His right hand there are pleasures for evermore. But God's pleasures can never come from inside an individual. They are *given*. Given from outside in. That is because God, from His fulness, delights to give of His fulness. The only way to receive it is to receive it. Then give it away, because receiving what is not ours and that we have not earned is glorified in giving it away. It is eternal pleasure to receive, and eternal pleasure to give it away. That is how the universe continues and survives and perpetuates itself. The God of Three cannot help but give. And there is no possibility that, in that respect, They can or will change. That is the way things are. That is the way things will always be.

There will never be eternal pleasure or eternal satisfaction outside those parameters. Surrender to Jesus is surrender to our Creator's rules. Submit and be blessed. Rebel and be crooked and cursed. Life on earth is the place, over our 70 allocated years, where all this is brought into sharp focus, and all decisions in relation to it are eternal - eternally upwards into glory or eternally downwards into everlasting pain. There are no alternatives, no other options. We must be our own Judge and Jury, before we stand before God's perfectly righteous Judge and Jury.

Earth is a bus stop. A place of transit. We were all born in a bus stop. We all know that. Time tells us that we are all on a journey, and everything else is passing us by. There might be a smidgen of shelter for a few of us for a little while, but the cold wind blows round our legs, and far too soon the rain gets in, soaking and freezing us. We all long for a warm, cosy, comfortable home that will never change and will give us shelter and love forever. Jesus came down from heaven to offer that home to each of us. He is the way, the only way. His is the only bus to catch. Although our destination does not arrive immediately, we know that His bus is safe, gives us shelter from much of the cold outside, and will certainly arrive at Home one eternal day. Soon, please, my amazing Friend.

Surrender, my wonderful fellow traveller of earth. Surrender and be blessed. I beg of you. Today, while you have the chance.

About the author.

Dick Bell was born in Kenya of a British family. His major love was aeroplanes, and, after his secondary schooling at Rossall in the UK, joined the RAF as a pilot. He became a Christian as a cadet at the RAF College Cranwell. He left the RAF after 20 years and became the main Bible Teacher at a Christian Conference Centre in Devon called Upcott, where he taught mainly children and teenagers for 26 years. He is married with one daughter and two grandsons. During his time at Upcott he took part in four Hovercraft expeditions on appropriate rivers across the world, under the leadership of Mike Cole OBE. Following the last expedition to Nicaragua, in 2000 he was called by God to take up full-time Missionary work there, where he founded the UK charity SIFT. His Missionary remit was four-fold – Initiate, Develop, Establish, Delegate. That enabled him to hand over the charity and begin a final new agricultural work on the Island of Ometepe in Nicaragua, where he also founded a new Church. He was prompted to write all the chapters in the Two-trees Series of books by the Holy Spirit since becoming a commuting Christian Missionary. He was granted an MBE in 2014 for his work in the Third World.

Titles of the Christian Booklets in
THE TWO TREES SERIES
by Dick Bell.

Book 1 – The Two Trees.

Book 2 – Christian Fundamentals.

Book 3 – All about Jesus.

Book 4 – Living Beyond the Drag Curve.

Book 5 – Farewell Adam.

Book 6 – Walking in the Spirit.

Book 7 – The Holy Spirit.

Book 8 – The Miracle of the Normal.

Book 9 – Creating New Heavens and New Earth.

Book 10 – The Eternal Diamond.

Book 11 – Justice and Rewards.

Book 12 – Heavenly Perspectives.

Book 13 – New Knowledge of Heaven.

Book 14 – Wonderful Youth.

Book 15 – Churches without Walls.

Book 16 – A Book of Meditations.

Book 17 – The Necessity of Prayer.

Book 18 – Relationships. God's Faithfulness.

Book 19 – Experiences.

Book 20 – God's Dolls House.

Book 21 – God the scientist.

Book 22 – My Personal Lifestyle.

Book 23 – A Book of Quotes.

Book 24 – The Chasm.

Book 25 – Some Deep Blessings from Jesus.

Printed in Great Britain
by Amazon

27544365R00037